BRIEF MEMOIR

OF

GEORGE MIFFLIN DALLAS,

OF

PHILADELPHIA.

PRINTED AT THE OFFICE OF THE SATURDAY EVENING POST, 66 SOUTH THIRD STREET.
PHILADELPHIA:
1853.

BRIEF MEMOIR

OF

GEORGE MIFFLIN DALLAS,

OF

PHILADELPHIA.

R. E. PETERSON & CO.
PHILADELPHIA :
1853.

GEORGE MIFFLIN DALLAS.

The citizen, whose name appears at the head of this article, was born in the city of Philadelphia, on the 10th day of July, 1792. At that time and several years afterwards, his father, the late Alexander James Dallas, held the office of Secretary of the Commonwealth, by the appointment of General Thomas Mifflin, the first Governor of Pennsylvania, under the constitution of 1790.

He was the second of three sons, the elder of whom was the late Commodore Dallas of the navy of the United States, and the younger, the late Judge Dallas of the city of Pittsburg. After the usual preparatory course of study, which he pursued at Germantown, under the superintendance of Mr. Dorfeuille, and at Philadelphia, under Provost Andrews, he entered Nassau Hall at Princeton, New Jersey, as a student of the arts and sciences, and after a residence of three years, was graduated with the highest honors of his class.

Towards this venerable institution, long and justly celebrated for the successful cultivation of literature and the sciences, Mr. Dallas has ever cherished a filial regard, while his subsequent career has given him rank among the most honorable and honored of her sons. Having completed his academical studies, he commenced with ardor the study of the law, in the office of his father, under whose tuition he rapidly acquired the elements of his future profession. His progress was suddenly interrupted by a great public event, which for a time disturbed the plans and diverted the pursuits of a large number of our citizens.

On the 18th of June, 1812, war was declared by the Congress of the United States, against the united kingdom of Great Britain and Ireland, and Mr. Dallas partaking largely of the patriotic feelings excited by that event, suspended his studies and joined a company of volunteers, with a view to military duty, intending to resume and complete his preparation for the bar, when his services as a soldier, should no longer be required. This purpose was, however, soon modified by an unexpected call upon him for patriotic service in another capacity. Albert Gallatin was about to proceed to Russia, upon the mission which issued in the treaty of Ghent; and having selected Mr. DALLAS to accompany him as private secretary, he was discharged from his military engagements, and a few days afterwards, left the United States on that mission. Previously to his departure, in April, 1813, and about three months before he attained the age of twenty-one years, he was admitted to the bar; the court consenting, in consideration of the peculiar circumstances, to relax their rules, both in respect to the time of preparatory study, and the age required for admission.

Here we must suspend our narrative, to introduce a brief account of the family to which Mr. DALLAS belongs: it will throw light upon our subject, and not be without interest to the reader. Robert Charles Dallas, the paternal grandfather of GEORGE MIFFLIN DALLAS, emigrated from Scotland to the Island of Jamaica, about the middle of the last century, or a little earlier. He was by profession a physician, and after a career of great success and reputation in that island, returned to Scotland, for the double purpose of regaining his health and educating his children. His family at that time, besides his wife, who survived him, consisted of four sons: Robert, Stuart, Alexander James, Charles—and two daughters—Charlotte and Elizabeth. Dr. Robert Charles Dallas did not return to Jamaica, although most of his children did. One or two of them settled in England. Of his immediate descendants, some have been highly distinguished as lawyers or authors. The late Chief Justice Dallas of the Common Pleas of England, belonged to the family.

Alexander James Dallas, the third son of Robert Charles Dallas, and the father of the subject of this memoir, was born in the island of Jamaica, on the 21st of June, 1759. Soon after his father's return to Scotland, he was placed at an academy in the neighborhood of London, under the care of the celebrated Elphinstone. While there, he attracted the notice of Dr. Samuel Johnson, also of Dr. Franklin, who occasionally visited his instructor. The death of his father, which soon occurred, interrupted his studies and clouded his prospects. Being compelled by his circumstances to provide for himself the means of support, he left the academy and enrolled his name in the Temple, as a student at law; but was soon induced, by what seemed to him, at that time an advantageous offer, to engage in a mercantile employment. He was destined, however, to another disappointment; as, after about two years laborious service as a clerk and accountant, his employer suddenly changed his pursuits and his country. Alexander James then returned to the home of his mother, where he resumed, under the direction of a private tutor, the studies which had been interrupted by his father's death. In 1780, being about twenty-one years of age, he was united in marriage to Arabella Maria Smith, a daughter of Major George Smith, of the British army. Soon after this event, he finally left England, intending to settle in the island of Jamaica; but owing to the climate and other causes, he soon resolved, in opposition to the remonstrances of his friends, to leave the dominions of Great Britain and fix his future residence in the United States. He arrived in the city of New York, early in June, 1783. From that city he proceeded to Philadelphia, then the seat of the national government, and on the tenth day after his first landing on the shores of the United States, took the oath of allegiance to the Commonwealth of Pennsylvania. The war of independence had in fact closed, although the treaty of peace was not signed until the third of September following.

Having acquired previously to his arrival in the United States, a sufficient knowledge of the law to commence the practice of it, and having attained the age of twenty-four years and taken the oath of allegiance to Pennsylvania, before the treaty of peace, he supposed there could be no objection to his immediate admission to the bar. The courts, however, anticipating perhaps, from the probable course of events, an inconvenient enlargement of the bar, modified their rules, a short time before his application, so as to require a residence of two years within the State, as a pre-requisite to admission. This unexpected obstacle diverted his energies for a short time to a new channel. His skill in accounts, acquired in the manner already mentioned, commended him strongly to Mr. Jonathan Burrall, a commissioner for settling the accounts of the Commissary and Quarter Master's Department of the revolutionary army, whose acquaintance he had casually made. An engagement with this gentleman, while it furnished him the means of support, also afforded an opportunity of more ample preparation for the active duties of his profession. He was admitted to the bar of the Supreme Court of Pennsylvania, on the 13th of July, 1785.

At that time the laws of Pennsylvania were not very clearly defined; but happily the administration of them was in the hands of men well qualified to delineate the outlines and lay the foundation of a system of jurisprudence suited to the wants of the people in their new political and social relations. It is scarcely possible to overrate the value of the services rendered to the people by the McKeans, the Wilsons, the Bradfords, Ingersols, Rawles, Lewis's, Tilghmans of the day and their compeers. The doctrines of the Declaration of Independence to become practical, required changes in the laws affecting the social as well as political relations. For the attainment of these objects, the virtues and abilities of such men, afforded a sufficient guaranty; and the part which Mr. Dallas performed in this delicate and difficult labor, was in no respect inconsiderable or unimportant. Within five years after his admission to the bar, he collected and prepared for publication a volume of cases, many of which were decided before the revolution: a service to the profession, and, we may say, to the law itself at that time, which we, at this day, can scarcely appreciate.

To his other duties, Mr. Dallas soon added the distracting one of politics. There were reasons at that time for connecting the study of political doctrines with the profession of the law, which are not so urgent or apparent now. The great principles of free government had indeed been settled, but nothing more. From these sprung spontaneously, other questions of absorbing interest. A confederation of the states had been formed, but it was defective both in its principles and details. The great national want of that day was, "a plan of more perfect union," which should "establish justice, ensure domestic tranquillity, provide for the common defence, promote the general welfare, and secure the blessings of liberty:" a great problem this, involving responsibilities, as vast as the national weal, and difficulties which, to be properly estimated, must be felt: so great indeed, that at this day, priceless as is the value of the Union, it would perhaps be impossible to overcome them. Besides, the constitutions of several of the states had been hastily formed: that even, which had been matured by the philosophical mind of Franklin, was destined to an early change. Few, if any of them, were even then, entirely satisfactory. Differences of opinion, naturally, not to say necessarily, existed. Earnest discussion followed, tending to conclusions, commensurate in importance and value, with the political institutions and constitutions in which they are embodied. Amid these events and under such dicipline, the political principles of Mr. Dallas were formed. They were the convictions of a vigorous, philosophical mind, deliberately adopted, after long, earnest and thorough debate, by men of uncommon power, upon the true nature of free government and of the American Institutions, considered as a means of perpetuating it. His political principles were therefore exclusively of American growth, and formed by the progress of events. They inclined him decidedly and strongly to enlarge, rather than restrain the limits of popular rights, and at a later period, determined, what may be called his party relations.

"The origin of the two permanent political parties is distinct as a matter of history, and is honorable in all its incidents. It preceded organization. The principles destined to agitate governments by their collision, were enunciated, before that government existed. Power was yet unknown. There was no court to propitiate; no club to terrify or excite; no treasure to covet; ambition was without an object; avarice without a bait; servility without an idol. The substitution of republicanism for monarchy had been almost an act of unanimity. All thirsted alike for liberty and order. Hence, the subsequent ripening of the federal constitution was chiefly an intellectual process, during which the wise and the virtuous differed as to the means of attaining the same end, without subjecting themselves for an instant, to the ordinary and odious imputations of intrigue, faction, interest or fear. Mind was at work, not on what then *was*, with countless, complicated and contradictory influences; but on what was *to be;* and in advance of every selfish motive and of every conscious bias, unfriendly to purely honest patriotism, the leading statesmen of that day promulgated with uncommon ability, their respective schemes of polity, developing their differences in struggles, which must always and unavoidably precede the creation of a new system. The manifest integrity and transcendent ability with which opposing views were maintained, inspired universal forbearance and respect; and the very compromises made to attain some definite result, attest the existence of principles, in themselves irreconcilable. Indeed it may be said, that what was thus early yielded, has tended to give greater identity of character to both parties, as well as more precision of purpose; and that each, in a natural and self-consistent course of action, has hitherto continued to avail itself of every opportunity to reclaim in practice, the concessions originally made in theory."

We here take occasion to say, that in this light, we ought to view some of the questions of our own times, which have been unduly agitated and not without danger to the Union: we allude to the compromises of the constitution and questions touching its construction. They are not new questions; nor has new light been thrown upon them, by more pure, patriotic, or philosophical minds. They were all considered, before the federal constitution was formed. They were definitely settled when that great act was adopted, and the faith of the states is solemnly pledged to maintain it, according to the terms and in the sense in which it was adopted.

This new form of national government, went into operation on the 4th day of March, 1789, and a new constitution for Pennsylvania in 1790, within seven years after Mr. Dallas acquired the right of

American citizenship. In the discussions which preceded the adoption of these two great instruments, he largely participated. In 1791, as already mentioned, he was appointed Secretary of the Commonwealth of Pennsylvania, under the new constitution, but without solicitation on his part. His professional and political exertions had already made him extensively known to the leading men of the nation, while his official position enlarged the circle of his personal acquaintance. Governor Mifflin was a man of revolutionary renown. He had been the first aid-de-camp of General Washington, a member of the old Congress, and for a time its president. In the city of Philadelphia, then the seat of the national and state governments, Mr. Dallas was the efficient and stirring spirit of the republican party; acting in unison with such men as Dr. James Hutchinson, Jonathan D. Sergeant, Geo. Bryan, Peter S. Duponceau, Thomas McKean, Edward Fox, John Barclay, Thomas Lieper, J. Swanwick, and others; to whom much more of fame and gratitude is due than has yet been awarded.

Upon the election of Jefferson, Mr. Dallas was appointed Attorney of the United States, for the Eastern District of Pennsylvania. He continued in this office until October 1814, when he was appointed Secretary of the Treasury of the United States, an office at that time beset with unusual difficulties and responsibilities. His character commanded the confidence, and his official conduct the approbation of the public.

About this time, the public career of George Mifflin Dallas may be said to have commenced. Conversant, from boyhood, with that circle of patriotic citizens in which his father most familiarly moved, he would naturally imbibe, from that source, even if there had been no other, impressions or views of politics, which in early manhood, could scarcely fail to ripen into principles. But these impressions and views were enforced and their bearing and importance explained by the precepts and example of one, who deserved and received from him the most profound reverence. His public life, from its commencement therefore, may be properly regarded as a carrying out, under new and diversified conditions of the country, the great principles of government which were fully settled upon, as early as the year 1801, and thenceforth adopted by the democratic party. This will appear as we proceed.

The occasion of Mr. Gallatin's mission to Russia, already alluded to, was the offer of the Emperor Alexander, to mediate between the United States and Great Britain. On his arrival at St. Petersburgh, he learned that Great Britain had declined the Emperor's offer. With a view to concert some other means of negociation, Mr. Dallas was sent by Mr. J. Q. Adams, (our minister at that court) and Mr. Gallatin, from St. Petersburgh to London, with despatches to Count Lieven, the Russian Ambassador at the Court of St. James; the Emperor of course, concurring in the measure. The particular object in view, was to ascertain through that medium, the wishes of the British government, and should they be favorable to peace, to settle upon a time and place for adjusting its terms. The overture thus made, resulted in the designation of Ghent as the place of negociation. To that place, after a short detention in England, Mr. Dallas repaired. The commissioners on the part of the British government, were Lord Gambier, Henry Gouldburn, and William Adams. On the part of the United States, Messrs. Adams, Gallatin, Bayard, Clay, and Russell. The negociation lasted a considerable time, but the details of it are foreign to our purpose. During a residence of several months, Mr. Dallas was in daily intercourse with those distinguished statesmen, and by his position and relations to the American Commissioners, enjoyed the best means of initiation into the mysteries of diplomacy;—an advantage of which he made the best improvement. Suddenly, however, and somewhat unexpectedly, he was required to return to the United States, as bearer of confidential despatches of great importance. Accordingly he embarked in the frigate John Adams, which had taken out Messrs. Clay and Russell, and arrived at New York in the latter part of October, 1814. Thence proceeding without delay to Washington, he executed his commission by delivering the documents entrusted to him, personally into the hands of President Madison. Mr. Dallas did not return to Ghent, but in November following, was appointed Remitter of the Treasury; an office which he held about a year and a half, when he resigned it and returned to Philadelphia, with a view to the more ordinary duties of his profession.

Before we pass on, a word or two, illustrative of the times and of the character of President Madison, may not be unacceptable to the reader. The despatches before mentioned, consisted of the famous preliminary propositions (*sine qua non,*) which Great Britain, through her commissioners, insisted on as indispensable to a treaty. The British army had about two months before destroyed the Capitol, the President's House, and the public offices. Mr. Dallas found the President residing in a private dwelling; his appearance was care-worn, and to the eye of a casual observer, would have seemed dejected. Withal he was suffering from a severe inflammation in the face, which he protected by a bandage. But the moment the despatches were put into his hands, he broke the seal, and at a glance comprehended their purport. Immediately his countenance lighted up and his whole manner changed. He rose quickly from his seat, and advancing towards Mr. DALLAS, remarked with great emphasis and animation, "These will do." "I hope so," replied Mr. DALLAS, "for I know their contents." "Yes, these will do," continued the President; "they will unite the American people, which is what we most need; no patriotic citizen of any party, will hesitate a moment, to reject conditions so extravagant and unjust."

So confident was the President of the correctness of this conclusion, that he ordered the immediate publication of these *sine qua non* propositions, departing on this occasion, from the established etiquette of diplomacy pending a negociation. Their effect on the public mind is well remembered.

The life of a lawyer, unless diversified by matters beyond his professional sphere, commonly contains but little to interest the general reader, yet it is undoubtedly true, that no secular employment requires a larger conception of nature, more various knowledge, or higher and more diversified intellectual endowments. A right conception of the true dignity of the bar, followed up by proper, well-directed, persevering efforts to attain it, constitute an excellent, if not the very best qualification for the wider sphere of legislation and political science. In this way, we may, to some extent, account for the fact, that so large a proportion of our eminent statesmen commence their career at the bar.

The qualifications of Mr. DALLAS for either sphere of activity, were uncommonly good. He had been prepared for the practice of the law, by the fond industry of his father, one of the most learned, laborious, and honored members of the Philadelphia bar; not less celebrated then, than now, for the thorough preparation and trial of causes. He had imbibed too, from the same source, a theory of politics, which first found its truest representative in Mr. Jefferson. This theory he set forth, at a later day, in an admirable discourse delivered in Philadelphia, on the centennial anniversary of the birthday of that distinguished man. Gifted with intellectual powers of a high order, improved by skilful and assiduous culture, with a copious and fluent diction, a cultivated and poetical taste, a dignified and graceful delivery—qualities which, while they attracted strongly the attention of his fellow citizens, enforced upon him the necessity of responding to their call, upon occasions of public interest. Such occasions were not unfrequent. The stirring events of the war, the divided state of public opinion, the acrimony of party spirit, and the connexion of his father with the administration of Mr. Madison, made it quite impossible, had he been so inclined, to confine his labors and pursuits to the halls of justice. Naturally, therefore, inevitably we might almost say—Mr. DALLAS from the beginning of his professional career, took a prominent and very decided part in the political agitations of the country.

On the 4th of July, 1815, within a twelvemonth after his return from Ghent, he delivered an oration at the invitation of his Democratic fellow citizens of the city and county of Philadelphia, in which he took occasion to review with great spirit the grounds of controversy between the United States and Great Britain, and to vindicate the policy and measures of our government. This was his first public appearance, so far as we can learn, in the arena of party politics. The effort attracted more generally and strongly, the favorable regard of the Democratic party towards him; which was not without advantage in the way of his profession. He was appointed the first Solicitor of the Bank of the United States, established by Act of Congress in 1816, which, considering the national character and the magnitude of the institution, was justly deemed an office of great importance. The policy of a National Bank, as a permanent institution, had not at that time been sufficiently considered; yet, as a temporary expedient against the extraordinary urgencies of the times, or, so to speak, as a *post war measure*, it was regarded with a degree of favor, and received a support from the Democratic party, which was afterwards withdrawn.

In 1817, Mr. DALLAS was appointed by the Attorney General, his representative in the City and County of Philadelphia. During the same year, he appeared as counsel, at the request of Governor Findlay, on his behalf, before the celebrated Committee of Inquiry. In the management of this affair, he displayed a degree of ability, which amply compensated for any lack of experience. The result fully justified the confidence reposed in one so young. These, however, are minor topics. Passing without note, several years of Mr. DALLAS' professional life, to the year 1824, near the close of Mr. Monroe's administration, we find him once more conspicuously active in promoting the election of General Jackson. Although he greatly admired the statesmanship and signal abilities of Mr. Calhoun, who had been nominated in several quarters for the office of President of the United States, yet, with a view to unite the whole Democratic party, he yielded his preference for the distinguished Carolinian, and with that gentleman's knowledge and assent, at a public meeting held in the city of Philadelphia, withdrew his name for that office, and proposed him as the candidate of Pennsylvania, for the office of Vice-President. This movement was enthusiastically seconded throughout the Union. Mr. Calhoun was elected to the office of Vice-President. General Jackson received only ninety-nine of the electoral votes—one hundred and thirty-one being necessary to a choice—yet fifteen more than Mr. J. Q. Adams received, and fifty-eight more than the number cast for Mr. Crawford.

The election of Mr. Adams by the House of Representatives, under these circumstances, gave occasion to a new and more decided expression of the popular sentiment; perhaps we should say, of the popular principle of our government. The disregard shown by the act, to the wishes of the greater number, naturally aroused the popular mind. Earnest discussions followed, in which Mr. Dallas took a prominent and decided part. The conclusions of the country on the whole matter, were expressed at the election of 1828, when Mr. Adams received eighty-three only of the electoral votes, and General Jackson one hundred and seventy-eight. To this result, the exertions of Mr. Dallas, particularly within his own State, largely contributed. The same year, Mr. Dallas was elected to the office of Mayor of the city of Philadelphia, an office, which of late years, has seldom been held by any citizen belonging to the same political party; but worthy of note, in this place, chiefly as an evidence of the enthusiasm and union of the party, produced, in no small degree, by his exertions during the Presidential canvass. This office he resigned in a short time, upon his appointment as Attorney of the United States for the Eastern District of Pennsylvania.

In 1831, Mr. Dallas was elected by the Legislature of Pennsylvania, to the Senate of the United States, to him a new sphere, and by its more ample scope, better suited to the exercise of his talents and diversified attainments.

The limits of so brief an article do not allow us to follow him, with much minuteness of incident in that dignified body. He participated frequently, and with marked ability, in debates on important questions, and on several exciting occasions, with singular effect, faithfully observing the instructions of the State he represented, whenever given. Thus, in obedience to repeated instructions of the Legislature of Pennsylvania, he supported the re-charter of the Bank of the United States, and a protective tariff; feeling himself in duty and conscience bound, whatever might be his private judgment, faithfully to represent his constituency. The same principle of action, he afterwards illustrated in another capacity, upon a memorable occasion which will be particularly noticed, yet not independently of other considerations of equal, if not paramount importance. His speech on apportioning the members of congress under the census of 1830, in opposition to a movement of Mr. Webster, was much spoken of at the time. It was a speech of great power, and produced the designed and desired effect. He also defended, in a speech of great eloquence and force, his personal friend, the late Edward Livingston, when that gentleman was nominated to the Senate by President Jackson, for the office of Secretary of State. The confirmation was strongly opposed both by Mr. Clay and Mr. Webster; but when Mr. DALLAS resumed his seat, these gentlemen—and it is due to their memory to mention the fact—promptly and magnanimously withdrew their opposition. About this time, the personal relations of Mr. DALLAS with President Jackson, became intimate and confidential; it was his happiness to enjoy the friendship of that distinguished man with unabated warmth, until his death.

The senatorial term of Mr. DALLAS expired on the 3rd of March, 1833. He peremptorily declined a reëlection, and immediately returned to his profession. Governor Wolf then tendered to him the office of Attorney General of the Commonwealth, and the office being congenial with his pursuits, he accepted and retained it, until the close of the administration of that excellent Chief Magistrate.

But another sphere of public service awaited him. In 1837 President Van Buren offered him a mission to the Court of St. Petersburgh, which (as before mentioned) he had visited in 1813, during the reign of Alexander. A better selection could not have been made to represent such a government as ours, at the Court of the Czar. His republican simplicity blended with personal dignity and elegance of manners required no adventitious aid on public occasions, to bar disparagement to himself or to his country. It is well known that this is the most splendid of the Courts of Europe. Magnificence, pomp, and the awe they inspire, seem to be regarded almost as a necessary means of government; and a departure from the established ceremonial, by an Ambassador, would be a singularity which could not fail to be generally remarked. But Mr. DALLAS, although moving amidst most gorgeous displays, during his residence at St. Petersburgh, never compromised upon any occasion the true dignity of an American citizen by an unnecessary departure from the simple habits and costume of his country. On the contrary, he scrupulously adhered to them whenever, and so far as was compatible with due respect to the

Emperor; and by this means, on more than one occasion, elicited unusual acts of courtesy from the monarch. The amicable relations, which then (and indeed ever have) subsisted between the two countries, gave little opportunity for the exercise of diplomatic skill. Yet, while ever watchful for the interests and dignity of his country, he had it in his power on several occasions materially to subserve the interests of Americans.

In 1839 he was recalled from this mission at his own request. Soon after his return to Philadelphia, the office of Attorney General of the United States (having become vacant, by the death of Mr. Grundy) was offered to him, by the President. For personal reasons, however, he declined it, and again resumed the practice of the law, mingling unostentatiously and quietly with his fellow citizens as before, in the walks of private and professional life; but he was not allowed to remain long in seclusion. In 1844 he was nominated by the Democratic party for the office of Vice-President of the United States, and in December of that year was elected to that high station.

Before we proceed to this part of the public life of Mr. Dallas, we crave indulgence for a few general observations which may seem quite common-place to the reader; yet, are important to be borne in mind by him, as he proceeds. The office of Vice-President of the United States, as it was conceived of by the framers of the Constitution, did not differ in its nature from the office of President. As that instrument was originally adopted, a Vice-President might be aptly described, as the second of two Presidents concurrently elected to one and the same office:—the priority of actual incumbency between them, being determined by the relative number of electoral ballots cast for each. Considered however as a *distinct* office, under the Constitution as amended in 1803, the Vice-President belongs exclusively to the executive branch of the government. It is true, by a special provision of the Constitution (even as originally adopted) the Vice-President presides over the senate, during the abeyance of his executive functions; yet without the power to participate in the debates of that body or to vote, except in the single case of an equal division of the Senators:—a case not likely to occur, except on doubtful or difficult questions, or such as involve controverted principles of public policy. This limitation of the power of the Vice-President, when thus acting, to what may be called the case of necessity, carries with it, by implication, a correlative and coördinate limitation upon the power of the Senators, individually and collectively, which although difficult to be enforced by Parliamentary means—owing to the nature of deliberative functions—nevertheless, cannot be disregarded, without a violation of the spirit of the Constitution. We mean, in brief, that Senators cannot rightfully, at pleasure, evoke the vote of the Vice-President by means of a factitious tie. The power itself, if not anomalous, is very peculiar. When exercised *to enact a bill* into a law, it mixes Executive with Legislative power, which the Constitution intends as far as possible, shall be kept distinct. When exercised *in the negative* upon questions exclusively within the cognizance of the Senate or upon bills which have passed the House of Representatives, it is in some respects comparable to the so-called *Veto* power of the President. It may have even a wider reach; for it may be exercised to defeat a bill of the House, founded upon the recommendation of the President; and thus produce an actual collision between executive powers, (Art. I. Sect. III. § 4: Art. II. Sect. III.)—a result, which the framers of the Constitution certainly could not have intended or even foreseen. No inconvenience, however, has ever arisen from this provision of the Constitution, or the actual exercise of the power thereby conferred. Thus far, it has always been lodged in the hands of wise and patriotic men; who, for the most part, have decidedly concurred in the policy and leading measures of the administrations, with which they were respectively connected. Indeed no case has yet arisen for its exercise, which could have led to any serious embarrassment, if we except one, which will presently be noticed.

Of the ability of Mr. DALLAS as a presiding officer, it is sufficient to say, that among the many distinguished Presidents of that august body, none has ever enjoyed in a larger measure, the respect and confidence of its members; or imparted by his presence and official decorum, greater dignity to their deliberations.

The most imposing scene which occurred during his Presidency, was witnessed in July, 1846, upon the final passage of the tariff act of that year. On that occasion, to employ the language of the author of the history of the Polk administration "he had an opportunity of illustrating his moral firmness of character, by an act of bold and majestic grandeur, which stamped him as one of the distinguished men of the age." This bill passed the House of Representatives on the 3d of July, 1846, by a vote of 114 to 95. It had been drawn in accordance with the recommendations of the President, and embodied principles which entered deeply into the Presidential canvass of 1844, in all parts of the country. When this bill was submitted to the final vote of the Senate, it appeared, that the Senators of eleven of the States were in favor of it; the Senators of eleven other of the States were opposed to it, while those of each of the remaining States, eight in number, were divided. Thus the bill was put in the power of the Vice-President, whose opinions, upon the particular provisions it contained, were, up to that moment, not certainly known. This circumstance alone, was calculated to add much to the interest already unusually great. Those who feared that local interests and feelings would imperceptibly bias the vote of the Vice-President, were indignant, that a great measure, founded upon a comprehensive view of the diversified interests of the Union, should be brought into peril, by the resignation of one of the Senators, and the refusal of another to vote for the bill, in obedience to the instructions of the State he represented. The suspense was, however, soon terminated. The Vice-President cast his vote in the affirmative, and the bill became a law.

Before proceeding to decide this most important question, he addressed the Senate in a brief but well considered speech, explanatory of the act he was about to perform. This was due to himself and to the country. "The scene," says the author just quoted, "was one of the most imposing that ever occurred in that chamber. The Representative Hall was almost deserted; the members crowded into the Senate, to witness the termination of the struggle. The galleries were crowded with beauty and fashion. The manufacturers were assembled in strong force—the Reporters bent eagerly forward to catch the words which fell from his lips. A solemn silence reigned. All eyes were turned on his commanding and expressive countenance, and each ear drank in the language of his celebrated address; which he pronounced with an earnestness and impressiveness of tone, which proved his sincerity."

To do justice to the occasion, as well as to the chief actor, we ought in this place to spread the address at length before the reader, but the limits allotted to this article, do not allow it; and we are constrained to refer him to the history of the times. It would not, perhaps, be extravagant to say, that never, at any other period, since the foundation of the American Union, have so important and diversified interests been poised upon a single vote. It changed at a breath a policy which had prevailed more than thirty years—a policy unequal in its operation, both upon States and individuals, and for that reason fraught with danger. It established a revenue system more productive to the National Treasury; less burthensome to the consumer; admitting of all necessary and just discriminations; yet bearing as lightly and equally as possible on every branch of industry, in all parts of the country.

There can be no reasonable doubt, that the influence of this change, by bringing the policy of the national government into closer harmony with the spirit of the constitution, has contributed to the greater solidity and strength of the Union. That such an act should have offended any class or portion of our patriotic citizens, (if not surrpising, owing to the tenacity with which men hold to their private interests,) can be accounted for only by inadequate views of the principles of the constitutional compact, or of the value of the Union, or the means indispensable to its continuance.

The dissatisfaction caused by this act of the Vice-President, was limited in extent, and ephemeral in duration. Experience, the great corrector of feeling, as well as of opinion, has set the seal of wisdom to the measure, and the increasing prosperity of the country, under the operation of the law, will add increasing strength to that code of political doctrines, of which Mr. DALLAS has ever been a zealous and powerful advocate.

During his Vice-Presidency, Mr. DALLAS prepared and published a letter on the project of a canal, from the southernmost part of the Gulf of Mexico, to the Tehuantepec Gulf on the Pacific shore; in which he discussed the whole subject of connecting the oceans through the Isthmus, and the practicability and peculiar advantages of the project mentioned, to the United States. The letter had the effect of drawing extensively public attention to the matter. The President was deeply impressed with the importance of the subject; took it into consideration, and gave instructions, which, had they been duly observed, would have resulted in the acquisition by treaty, of a right for the transit of the vast and increasing commerce of the United States, by the way which nature seems to have designed. In this production of his pen, as in many others, it is easy to discern the opinions of Mr. DALLAS, upon the expansive power of the American institutions, and their capability of adaptation through a progressive and natural development, to the full extent of their destined area.

In private life, Mr. DALLAS is easy of access and courteous to the humblest of his fellow citizens. Although few men have been distinguished by so many high official trusts, still fewer have borne their honors with so much republican simplicity; or at their exit from office, have assumed more readily, or with better grace, the unaffected deportment of a private citizen. Although his professional career has been so much interrupted by public cares, he ranks as a lawyer, with the most eminent of the profession. As an advocate, he is graceful, dignified, and uncommonly effective. Withal, he has found occasional

3

opportunities to indulge in literary pursuits, a taste for which he seems to have inherited. We might here refer to his published orations and addresses, as the productions of finished scholarship; but we prefer closing this article, by transcribing a poetical effusion, illustrative of a trait of his character not yet noticed. To some of our readers it will not be new, as it appeared a few years ago in a morning paper of Philadelphia. Yet those who best know Mr. DALLAS, will not easily believe, that it was written for any eye, beyond the domestic circle of which it is his highest earthly happiness to be the beloved and revered head.

TO MY WIFE.

SENT WITH MY PORTRAIT ON THE TWENTY-EIGHTH ANNIVERSARY OF MY WEDDING DAY.

1.

By truthful Sully sketch'd, how plain appears
The change produced, by eight and twenty years!
Sophia! mark that dimming eye;
The rigid brow of care;
The fallen cheek's ungenial dye;
Those folds of whiten'd hair;
How well in unison they chime
The triumph of remorseless Time!

2.

The outward casket these—whose depths enclose
A Gem, which never flaw nor fading knows:
What if old age, invite decay,
And form and feature wane,
That Gem, tho' all its case give way,
Will sparkling still remain,
Within enshrined from changing free,
Undying glows the *Love of Thee!*

3.

Harmless and vain, Time's breakers seem to roll
O'er that one treasure, seated in the soul!
The gift that youthful fondness gave
With cloudless heart and brow,
Tho' age hath made me grey and grave,
That gift I give *thee now*;
Myself with equal faith bestow,
As eight and twenty years ago!

www.ingramcontent.com/pod-product-compliance
Lightning Source LLC
LaVergne TN
LVHW020634110826
845149LV00004B/1193

* 9 7 8 1 4 1 8 1 9 1 4 3 6 *